B[.]
TO THE
TABLE

A 60-DAY JOURNEY

PASTOR JOHN R. ADOLPH
BISHOP DAVID L. TOUPS

Library of Congress Catalog Number: APPLIED FOR

Name: Adolph, John R., Author
              Toups, David L., Author
Title: *Back to the Table: A 60-Day Journey*
              Dr. John R. Adolph
              Bishop David L. Toups
              Advantage Books, 2023
Identifiers: ISBN Paperback: 978159757658
              ISBN eBook: 978159757757
Subjects: Books › Religion › Worship & Devotion Devotionals
              Books › Religion › Worship & Devotion Inspirational
              Books › Religion › Worship & Devotion Prayer

First Printing: October 2023
23 24 25 26 27 28   10 9 8 7 6 5 4 3 2 1

Acknowledgments

By Dr. John R. Adolph
Pastor, Antioch Missionary Baptist Church

Not long ago, while sharing lunch with my dear friend and brother, Bishop Toups, he made a remark that captured my soul and arrested my intellect. He said, "Pastor Adolph, I plan to introduce some new lessons for my Diocese, and they will be entitled 'Back to the Table'! As soon as he said it, my comment was a meaningful palindrome that I'm known for using when something strikes oil in the fertile ground of my mind. I said "WOWOWOWOWOWOWOW!" It was at that moment that this work had its genesis. It wasn't as if we sat at lunch to devise an excellent idea for a Christocentric anthology that would bless the community in which we live. It rose like the sweet smell of a pound cake baking in the oven for us not to miss.

With this in mind, I must pause and thank our Lord and Savior Jesus Christ for the inspiration He gave my brother, The Right Reverend Bishop David L. Toups. This work would have never been manifested if Bishop had held his peace that day. I'm so thankful we had time to chat before we got to the grilled salmon that had found our plates that day. Had we dined first, our discussion about the "the table" would have possibly been clouded by the delicious meal that came from it.

I also want to share a word of thanks to those persons who have worked behind the scenes to cause resources like this to come to fruition. In this stead, I thank God for Sister Larissa Martinez, the Administrative Assistant to Bishop Toups, who took his handwritten notes and produced one of the finest manuscripts ever. Thank you to my Executive Director, Minister Brooklyn Williams, for helping Bishop Toups and me organize, develop, and implement such a work.

And, I must share a very personal note of thanks to my dear friend and brother, Mr. Wayne Reaud, whose "table of the Christian faith, friendship, and brotherhood" has afforded me the honor and privilege of meeting wonderful people like Bishop Toups.

Bishop and I agree that what you now hold in your hand is far from a Pulitzer Prize award-winning bestseller. It is much more like a few scattered notes from the pens of two preachers who love God and the communities that we are privileged to serve. Yet this book is one of the most unique works ever published. Never before in the history of our municipality has a Catholic Bishop and a Baptist Pastor produced a Christo-centric anthology like this one. So enjoy it! Have fun with it! It's about faith, family, and unity in our community. Take the journey with us! Welcome BACK TO THE TABLE!

Introduction

By Bishop David L. Toups
Diocese of Beaumont

Thank you for picking up this little book about getting back to the table. Pastor John Adolph of Antioch Missionary Baptist Church and I have collaborated to offer simple, scriptural reflections to help you journey for 60 days and reflect on this important message.

In Southeast Texas we are a believing community, a family of faith. Our hope is that two shepherds from different Christian traditions are able to model the importance of working together for the common good. We truly love, respect, and appreciate each other.

By focusing on the different tables that appear in the Scriptures, we hope to reinforce the importance of getting back to the table: the table of the family and the table of the Lord. Repetition is the mother of learning, and so these 60 reflections are meant to drive home the importance of getting back to the table.

We believe that getting the families of our community to sit down at least 2 to 3 days a week can transform and lay a solid foundation for both marriages and children. There are so many obstacles to family life that we hope this book serves as a reminder of how essential getting back to the table is for the future of our civil society.

The second step of our campaign is to do our very best to get people back to the table of the Lord, back to church. In a post-Covid world, we need to be reminded of the essential nature of Christian community and fellowship, and the nourishment that the Lord Jesus desires to give us at His table every Sunday.

I am so grateful to my brother, Pastor Adolf, for wanting to do this project together. Our prayer is that our collaboration reminds the community of the importance of working together in our beautiful multicultural family of faith. May Southeast Texas continue to grow in the image and likeness of Christ as we work to build up the Kingdom of God for our good and the good of all His Church!

Day 1

GUESS WHO'S COMING TO DINNER
Dr. John R. Adolph

"Then Jesus six days before the Passover, came to Bethany, where Lazarus was, which had been dead, whom he raised from the dead" (John 12:1).

The dinner invitations have gone out; your name is on the list. The host is no ordinary host. The host for this table is like none other. Our host is the King of kings, the Lord of lords, the God of the galaxy, the Architect and Engineer of the universe! God is calling us back to the table to promote Christian love, unity, harmony, synergy, togetherness, oneness, and faith. Please take a moment and read St. John 12:1. It is the story of what occurs after Lazarus has been resurrected from the dead. In this narrative, a dynamic table is present that the Lord invites one man to. It is a communal table of inclusion, diversity, community, equity, and wholeness. In this stead, this passage beckons its reader to ponder the query, "Guess who's coming to dinner?" We know for sure that Lazarus accepted the invite. However, here is a devotional question we can begin our time together just thinking about. If God designed, developed, and redemptively deployed a table of Christian brotherhood that brought together Christians from every denomination, Catholics and Protestants, could He count on you to be present? Here's the excellent news of the day: If this book is in your hands, you are on God's invitation list! The prayer is that you accept the invite so you can join us at the table for dinner.

Day 2

WASTING TIME TOGETHER
Bishop David L. Toups

"A woman came to Him with an alabaster vial of very costly perfume, and she poured it on His head as He reclined at the table" (Matthew 26:7).

The purpose of the Back to the Table initiative is to remind us to "waste time" with our families and with God.

The woman who anointed Jesus' head was accused of throwing money away and being wasteful, yet what she did for Our Lord brought Him great comfort and joy as He knew His passion was drawing closer.

Taking the time to eat as a family or even time in church on Sunday might seem unproductive. Just think of how many more things you could be doing! Yet nothing is more precious than the gift of time you give one another by sitting down at table together several days a week. This is where life is shared, stories are told, jokes are made, tears are shed, and even a few arguments may be had – but this is how we grow in relationship with one another and strengthen family life.

Similarly, our Sunday worship is where we grow in relationship with God and our community of faith. But what a seeming waste! You could be playing sports, going to the movies, or sleeping in! Jesus invites us to "waste time" with Him and those we love, and that is truly time well spent! Let's get back to the table!

Day 3

OUR MAIN COURSE FOR THE EVENING WILL BE LAMB
Dr. John R. Adolph

"There they made him a supper; and Martha served: but Lazarus was one of them that sat at the table with him" (John 12:2).

palate

Every real table where food will be served reaches beyond pallet teasers, snacks, and appetizers to the main course. Don't you love the sound of that....the main course? It suggests that something amazing is about to take place. It carries with it a raison d'etre of sorts. It means that the chef has outdone himself, and the real reason for gathering at the table is about to be presented. You see, the main course is not an ala carte side order. It is the masterpiece of all that the kitchen has to offer. In John 12:1-2 Jesus invites his dear friend Lazarus, who has just been resurrected from the dead, to the table. On this particular day, the Jews prepare for the Passover, which can only mean one thing. The main course will be the Lamb (Ex. 12)! In the life of the Christian, our Lamb is heaven's main course. He alone provides the redemptive synergistic cohesiveness that unites Catholics and Protestants worldwide. He is not some ala carte side order or a snack before the meal. He is what makes the table amazing! Without Him, we have nothing. With Him, we have it all! Now, thank God for giving us His only begotten Son, Jesus Christ, our vicarious victorious eternal Lamb! For the Christian, regardless of denomination, He is our main course!

Day 4

ACCEPTANCE OF OTHERS
Bishop David L. Toups

"Now when He had spoken, a Pharisee asked Him to have lunch with him; and He went in, and reclined at the table" (Luke 11:37).

The vast majority of Jesus' ministry happens at the table. It is in the course of a meal that He teaches us over and over the lessons of life. In this Gospel passage, Jesus wants to remind us that we are to treat others the way we want to be treated – the Golden Rule! He accepts invitations from both the righteous and the sinner, for to Him all are brothers and sisters. He can converse with people whose opinions He disagrees with, and that is something our divided world could learn from. Jesus' humility allows Him to listen lovingly and accept the other where they are, while at the same time encourage better behavior. Picture our Lord's engagement with whomever He is dining. Am I such an attentive listener, or am I stuck in my own head thinking about what I am going to say next?

Coming back to the table means more than eating food, it is about receiving the other person into our hearts as we make ourselves humbly available to them.

Day 5

A TABLE AT A TIME LIKE THIS?
Dr. John R. Adolph

"There they made him a supper; and Martha served: but Lazarus was one of them that sat at the table with him" (John 12:2).

The scene in this pericope is dramatic. Reading it with your imagination would marvel something from a Stephen Spielberg film. Lazarus has been dead for four days, and Jesus shows up, commands that the huge boulder be moved, and then calls Him by his name…."Lazarus, come forth!" And the dead man hears the voice of His Lord and returns to life. The crowd is stunned, critics are silenced, doubters start believing, and the news quickly spreads that Jesus has done it again! Guess what happens next? Take a moment and read John 12:1-2 to get the answer right. Jesus takes Lazarus to a table. Why a table at a time like this? The answer is simple. Jesus brings Lazarus to the table because dead men don't eat. The point here is profound and prolific. Proof of being alive is that you belong at a communal table where life in Christ is celebrated and shared. This is why, as believers in the Lord, we must push, promote, and promulgate tables of Christian brotherhood everywhere. And, if you come across someone who does not want to join you at a table like this, remember the principle Jesus taught in this one story: Dead men don't eat! You must be made alive in Christ to love a table like this.

Day 6

THE SHEPHERD WHO FEEDS
Bishop David L. Toups

"You prepare a table before me in the presence of my enemies; You have anointed my head with oil; My cup overflows" (Psalm 23:5).

By far one of the most loved scriptures is Psalm 23. It is filled with comfort and hope, peace, and tranquility, and such beautiful pastoral imagery that speaks to our hearts. The "table of plenty" is presented to us as the way our Good Shepherd wants to feed us. God's desire to nurture and nourish us in abundance is so clear as He prepares the table, anoints our heads, and gives us drink to overflowing. Our world is starving for God, hungering, and thirsting for spirituality, and so often desperately trying to feast on the empty calories of the world that do not ultimately satisfy.

Let's lead our friends and family back on to the shoulders of the Good Sheperd and back into the flock of Christ. We know that it is only in going back to the table of the Lord that our souls will find rest and satisfaction.

Day 7

A TESTIMONY FROM THE TABLE
Dr. John R. Adolph

"Then Jesus six days before the Passover came to Bethany, where Lazarus was, which had been dead, whom he raised from the dead" (John 12:1)

One of the most incredible things that can take place at any table is table talk. You know, chatter that matters. Communal conversation, if you will. In short, the table does not just feature food; it also fosters fellowship. And fellowship brings to the table things that we talk about. During table talk, we often hear about politics, people, communal problems, etc. But the most fascinating part of table talk is when people start sharing their testimonies. During moments of discussion like this, you hear the news about the surgery that went well, the tumor that somehow disappeared, or even the health of a friend that was restored. Such was the case with Lazarus. He is at the table, and his testimony is so great that he never says a word, or at least nothing is recorded in scripture. This is due to the case that everyone in town knew that he was dead. Seeing a dead man at the table alive was testimony enough. Here's a great devotional moment for you to consider. What's your testimony? Has God ever done anything for you worth sharing with others? Share that news at the table, and if your miracle is great, show up! Your being present is a testimony all by itself.

Day 8

THE LAST SUPPER
Bishop David L. Toups

"When He had reclined at the table with them, He took the bread and blessed it, and breaking it, He began giving it to them" (Luke 24:30)

Jesus knew that His hour had arrived for His passion, and the most important thing to Him was to take time to spend with those closest to Him. At some point in time, we have all been invited to reflect about being on our deathbed and ask ourselves the question: should I have spent more time at work or with my loved ones. We all know the answer to this basic question. "Back to the Table" reminds us to not neglect those around us, even when other apparent goods come along like work or sports. Jesus knew that "reclining at table" was the most important thing He could do to show His love to His friends. It was at this same Last Supper that he told them. "There is no greater love than to lay down your life for your friends" (Jn. 15:13). Jesus was about to lay down His life on the Cross, but before that He wanted to give His friends life by His presence at the table. And that is a Presence that continues in the Eucharist as He "reclines at table" with us every Sunday. Let's get back to the table of our family and the table of the Lord.

Day 9

HE DID IT JUST FOR ME
Dr. John R. Adolph

"There they made him a supper; and Martha served: but Lazarus was one of them that sat at the table with him" (John 12:2)

Friends, if we know nothing else about God, we know this: God is a God of blessing. With this in mind, consider that there are two realms of blessing: indirect and direct. An indirect blessing is when God blesses you because you are attached to something or someone else who is blessed. For example, you have a best friend who just won the power ball, and they bless you with a bit of cash because they have it to spare. The blessing of the money fell into their lap, but because you are connected to them, you get some money, too. However, there are other times when God blesses you directly! God says, through His sovereign decision, I am doing this just for you! This is the blessing in the passage. You see, the meal that was fixed was prepared just for Lazarus. With this in mind, Lazarus has a right to exclaim with vigor, "He did it just for me!" Here's an excellent question for Christians who know the benefit of being at the Lord's table: Has God ever done anything that made you see that it was just for you? Your money could not buy it, your credit could not charge it, your checks could not write it, but God graced you with it. Remember this: Such blessings come to you so you will know what His grace tastes like. When moments like this happen, you owe the table a report saying, "He did it just for me!"

Day 10

REAL PRESENCE
Bishop David L. Toups

"While they were eating, Jesus took some bread, and after a blessing, He broke it and gave it to the disciples, and said, "Take, eat; this is My body." And when He had taken a cup and given thanks, He gave it to them, saying, "Drink from it, all of you;" (Matthew 26:26-27)

In our Catholic Tradition, we believe that Jesus is present at every Mass not only as the Word of God is proclaim and preached, but in a very particular way on the Altar/Table of the Lord. As He said those words 2000 years ago "this is my Body, this is my Blood", we believe that He is really present in the Eucharist to feed, nourish, and heal us every Sunday. Now that is a table worth getting back to!

Regardless of our denominational background, Jesus so wants to be with us, love us, comfort us, and so why would we shut Him out and not accept the gifts He wants to pour out upon us in His Word, His Sacrament, and in His Community.

Day 11

KINFOLKS AND FRIEND FOLKS THAT ARE GOOD FOLKS
Dr. John R. Adolph

"There they made him a supper; and Martha served: but Lazarus was one of them that sat at the table with him" (John 12:2)

The Washington family has a rich tradition. When it is your birthday, the entire family gathers, sits you in the birthday seat, makes a special cake, and sings Happy Birthday to you! Even though it is not his birthday, this passage gives a feeling of a unique celebration; after all, he was dead and is now alive. Lazarus had two sisters, Mary and Martha. Both of them were at the table after his marvelous resurrection. In short, they were kinsfolk that were good folks. The report from the passage is that Martha was serving the entire time. Isn't that a great report? It is not a party for her, but she is so excited that she lends her service to help celebrate her brother's life, who was dead but is now alive. You know such is true for believers in Christ, and it is why the table is so important. We gain the value and virtue of celebrating others and not only ourselves. Let's address the enormous pink gorilla sitting at this table quickly; some people can only celebrate when the celebration is for them. Here's some good Christ-centered advice: get past you and learn to celebrate others. Life in Christ is not just about you. It is about sharing special moments with kinsfolk and friend-folks who are good folks.

Day 12

CHILDREN'S TABLE
Bishop David L. Toups

"But she answered and said to Him, "Yes, Lord, but even the dogs under the table feed on the children's crumbs." Mark 7:28

Remember Thanksgiving as a kid? There was the adult table and the kid's table. The adult table always looked so much better with china and sliver wear, fancy goblets, and better food. The kids table had solo cups and chicken nuggets on paper plates. The adult table was the destination that one day you just knew you were going to get to.

Similarly, Jesus speaks to a woman who was a foreigner who didn't "belong" at the same table as the Jews. She reminds Him as she begs for the healing of her daughter that even the little dogs are fed by the children. She too deserved a morsel as she begs to grow closer to Jesus. She knows that at the kids table will the little dog will be fed by the morsels coming from the hands of the children (as kids always do!). Our Lord cannot but help to be moved by her faith even though she was from another "table". Jesus will eventually teach us that He came to seek and save all the Gospel and salvation are offered to all peoples. He desires us to come to the Table, and as we work together from our various churches and backgrounds, we grow closer together and do our part to build up the Kingdom of God.

Day 13

THERE'S STILL SOME SEATS OPEN AT THE TABLE
Dr. John R. Adolph

"There they made him a supper; and Martha served: but Lazarus was one of them that sat at the table with him" (John 12:2)

As you read the Holy Scriptures, you will notice that there are times when we have presented facts that need to be better defined. These are figures of speech called exclusive relativisms. We have one mentioned in the story of John 12. You see, we know that there is a table in the text. We also know that other guests are at the table to include Jesus. The exclusive relativism is that we must determine exactly how many seats were available that day. Excessive relativism aims to extend what you see existing because the apparent offer still stands. With this in mind, the most significant news of this story is that the same table that Lazarus was invited to share still has seats available for others to join us. In short, the same grace that God has showered Lazarus with was given to you, and if you have received it, it is also available to the whosoever will of the Lord's cross. To be sure, it is a blessing to have you at the Lord's wonderful merciful table. The question that we now must consider is who do we know that should be at the table that at present is missing? Here's a great redemptive activity for you to practice as we return to the table; invite them! Ask someone to join you as you pray, read, and study. And, if they do not know our Host, introduce them to Him! After all, there's none more remarkable than our Lord, Jesus Christ.

Day 14

EARLY CHURCH
Bishop David L. Toups

"And they devoted themselves to the apostles' teaching and fellowship, to the breaking of bread and the prayers" (Acts 2:42).

This is one of my favorite verses from the Acts of the Apostle. In one short verse it describes how the early church worshiped and how we still do today. In our Catholic Tradition, we have two parts to our Mass: the Liturgy of the Word and the Liturgy of the Eucharist. Acts 2:42 tell us they devoted themselves to the "apostles teaching and fellowship". We gather and break open the Word every Sunday. We all feast sumptuously on the Bible in all of our denominations as the

Lord feeds our souls.

The verse then continues to describe the gathering as "the breaking of the bread and the prayers." The "breaking of the bread" was an early title for the Eucharistic gathering referring back to Jesus' gestures of "taking blessing and breaking" as well as the Emmaus story when they recognized the Risen Christ in "the breaking of the bread" (Luke 24; 13-35).

As they did then, so we do now as we go back to the table of the Lord every weekend.

Day 15

WALK IT LIKE I TALK IT
Dr. John R. Adolph

"And the Lord said, Simon, Simon, behold, Satan hath desired to have you, that he may sift you as wheat: But I have prayed for thee, that thy faith fail not: and when thou art converted, strengthen thy brethren" (Luke 22:31-32)

At every table, there will be subjects that divide us, and there will be pertinent matters that unite us. One common thread that connects us every single time is the subject of human difficulty, harm, and hurt. Suffering is an all-inclusive allowable that somehow finds us all. In this passage, Jesus warns Simon at a table that a storm is brewing with his name on it and is heading in his direction. When Hurricane Ike showered the Gulf Coast with rain waters that rose to a record-breaking fifty-seven feet high, our communities hurt and brought us together like no other time. The storm felt like an enemy attack yet help came to our region wrapped in strange packages. One day, a group of skinheads bearing insignia from the racist, fascist Arian Nation from Baton Rouge stopped by a local Black church to offer them some assistance. You can only imagine how this was initially received, right? The skinheads prepared lunch for over eight hundred volunteers and hungry people. That's right, they prepared a table! The group leader, wearing a swastika sticker tattooed on his head, said, "There comes a time when we have to look beyond our bent philosophies and just be Christians who help each other get through hard times. It is easy for to talk it, but it means more when we walk it." Here's the truth: We cannot avoid human suffering, but we can gain strength from the table to help us endure it.

Day 16

THY KINGDOM COME
Bishop David L. Toups

"...and just as My Father has granted Me a kingdom, I grant you that you may eat and drink at My table in My kingdom, and you will sit on thrones judging the twelve tribes of Israel" (Luke 22:29-30).

Are you ever sharing a meal with family and friends, and you think to yourself "this is just perfect" or "I wish this moment just wouldn't end"? Well, that is a foretaste of the Kingdom of Heaven where everything just feels right, when we are in right relationship with everyone at the table, no one is bickering, and our hearts are completely satisfied. That feeling, this side of Eternity doesn't happen often, but when it does it is heavenly.

Our lives should yearn for Heaven and we should strive even now to experience that foretaste of the banquet by working to heal broken relationships, bring people together and gather as communities of faith every Sunday. Thy Kingdom come, thy will be done, on earth as it is on Heaven!

Day 17

SLICING AND DICING AIN'"T ALWAYS A GOOD THING
Dr. John R. Adolph

"And the Lord said, Simon, Simon, behold, Satan hath desired to have you, that he may sift you as wheat: But I have prayed for thee, that thy faith fail not: and when thou art converted, strengthen thy brethren" (Luke 22:31-32)

In the culinary sense, slicing and dicing can be a real blessing. To slice a piece of pound cake can be a real treat. To dice a carrot can make a pot of stew delicious. But slicing and dicing is not always good, especially if you are the object being sliced and Satan is the one holding the knife. Don't stop reading this article; it is just getting good! In this passage, Jesus warns Peter that satan wants to sift him as wheat. In our culture, we think that fruits and vegetables come from the grocery store, so this issue of sifting means little to us. However, realistically, it really suggests that Satan wants to slice and dice Peter. Satan wants Peter's life in pieces. Here's a great devotional query for us to ponder today. Have you ever seen a season of sifting where you felt everything had fallen to pieces? If you answered yes, you stand with an entourage of believers that can say to the Lord, "...though He slay me, yet will I trust Him." An ever more significant question beckons to be considered at this point. Did you have a table of support to strengthen you along the way? Here's the truth: God provides a table for us in tough times so that we keep the courage to fight on. It's a communal table with doctors, nurses, family, friends, and those who know the feeling and can help you.

Day 18

ALL ARE WELCOME
Bishop David L. Toups

"The kingdom of heaven may be compared to a king who gave a wedding feast for his son. And he sent out his slaves to call those who had been invited to the wedding feast, and they were unwilling to come" (Matthew 22:2-3).

Jesus broke lots of social barriers during His life and ministry. He wants all to know of His Love and the saving message of the Gospel. In this passage, the first to be invited rejected the generous invitation of the King and so he sent His servants to the highways and byways, or as Pope Francis reminds us, to the peripheries of society, to give everyone the chance to dine sumptuously with Him. Think about how each of us are called to fulfill the Third Commandment by keeping holy the Sabbath. Sunday Worship is the preeminent way we do this. Let's not reject the invitation of our King to this feast, but rather humbly and gratefully embrace the gift He gives us to come to His Table.

Day 19

SECRETS FROM THE TABLE THAT CAN SAVE YOU
Dr. John R. Adolph

"And the Lord said, Simon, Simon, behold, Satan hath desired to have you, that he may sift you as wheat: But I have prayed for thee, that thy faith fail not: and when thou art converted, strengthen thy brethren" (Luke 22:31-32)

Whenever a Christian goes through a season of suffering, there is a question we are known for asking God from time to time. Not every believer raises this question to the Lord, but many of us do. The existential ontological interrogative is to ask the Lord, "Why?" Have you ever been here before? Why the diagnosis? Why the death in the family? Why the loss of the job? Why the divorce? Why the trouble, trials, tragedies, and difficulties? The first thought that comes to mind is that it must be some form of punishment. We conclude that God is angry with us, and to express His anger and discontent, He allows us to suffer. However, if you sit at the table long enough, you find nothing could be further from the truth! In the passage mentioned above, Peter will be attacked by Satan, and the Lord does not stop it. The Lord allows it. But why, you ask? The news from the table informs us that when Satan gets our lives to fall to pieces, we have a redeemer who takes the broken pieces and designs a masterpiece! Here's a secret that can save you: God is too good to be bad, too sweet to be sour, and too kind to be mean. What you see as punishment is preparation; what you feel is a heavy burden will later be your blessing in disguise; your being cut could reveal your calling, and your period of trials build your trust in the Lord.

Day 20

COME UP HIGHER
Bishop David L. Toups

"And He began speaking a parable to the invited guests when He noticed how they had been picking out the places of honor at the table, saying to them" (Luke 14:7).

When we are at the table with our family and friends, are we there to be served or to serve. How great it is when everyone at table is aware of the needs of those around them; offering food dishes, pouring drinks, clearing plates, and eventually helping to wash the dishes. Think how wonderful the person who has just cooked the meal will feel as he/she sees the family cooperate around the table.

"Come up higher" will be experienced by the family that puts the needs of the other first. Jesus reminds us that He came "to serve and not be served" (Mark 10:45).

Since this selflessness is not always instinctual, we must ask for the grace to have a servant's heart and start teaching this virtue of service/charity to our children at a young age.

As we get back to the table, let's come as servants of one another.

Day 21

PRAYERS FROM THE TABLE THAT CHANGE EVERYTHING
Dr. John R. Adolph

"And the Lord said, Simon, Simon, behold, Satan hath desired to have you, that he may sift you as wheat: But I have prayed for thee, that thy faith fail not: and when thou art converted, strengthen thy brethren" (Luke 22:31-32)

Imagine sitting at a table with Jesus, and suddenly, He's not just talking to you in general. He's now talking directly to you. He informs you that Satan wants to get his narrow, nasty hands on you so that he can cause all kinds of trouble. A flutter rises from the bottom of your stomach, and your mind tries to think of what the enemy will attack next. Will it be your health, wealth, family, or faith? Will it be your future, your forward progress, or will he cause various facets of your life to fail, flop, and flounder uncontrollably? And while your mind starts to worry and wonder, you hear your Lord's comforting words that change everything. He says, "But I have prayed for you...." This is what Peter encountered that day with Jesus at the table. It wasn't the prayer for the food that blessed him; it was the prayer for his faith that kept him going. In short, the Lord affirms for Peter that He will not leave you during your season of trial. It will be then that my prayers to my Heavenly Father will be most evident in your life. Have you ever heard someone pray for you? What did you think or feel? What were you going through at the moment? Here's the bottom line: Prayers from the table often change everything!

Day 22

BLESSED ARE WE
Bishop David L. Toups

"When one of those who were reclining at the table with Him heard this, he said to Him, 'Blessed is everyone who will eat bread in the kingdom of God!'" (Luke 14:15)

Getting back to the table is preparing us for the blessedness of the Kingdom. Gathering at the table with our families and being a part of our faith communities molds our hearts more and more into the Heart of Christ.

Doesn't it make sense that these two simple activities bless us incredibly. Making the time to gather with family and faith community might seem to be unattainable. You might ask, how can I afford to take the time to do this? Well, the reality is, how can you afford not to? May our eyes be opened to realize that getting back to the table is transformative for our families and communities. As St. John Paul II reminded us, it is nothing less than about the future of humanity itself: "the future of humanity passes by way of the family."

Day 23

THE TABLE ISN'T JUST ABOUT FOOD IT'S REALLY ABOUT YOUR FAITH

Dr. John R. Adolph

"And the Lord said, Simon, Simon, behold, Satan hath desired to have you, that he may sift you as wheat: But I have prayed for thee, that thy faith fail not: and when thou art converted, strengthen thy brethren" (Luke 22:31-32)

What comes to mind when you hear the word table? Food! But we seldom think about our faith. Here's the absolute truth: the Bible declares that "Faith cometh by hearing, and hearing by the Word of God" (Romans 10). When you find a seat at the Lord's table of communal brotherhood, you are there to have your faith fed. Here's our problem: We feed our faith once a week with a twenty-minute sermon and complain that it needs to be shorter. We then turn around and feed our flesh like crazy. When our tests and trials come, our flesh often wins while our faith sometimes fails. At the table in the text, Jesus is through serving bread and wine. He is now serving Word ala carte. Here's the Word for Peter and every Christian "....that your faith fail not." The meaning of this is so rich. The term fail comes from the Greek term eclipto. We borrow our term eclipse from it. You see, during an eclipse, whether solar or lunar, you end up separated from the sun. Hear the soul food message of Jesus from this table! Hey Christians, during seasons of trial, do not let anything separate you from Me! Why? You can do nothing without me, but you can do everything with me! If you're currently going through a trial, consider this devotional to be a whisper from God that says, "Stay with me; I've got you covered!"

Day 24

BE PREPARED
Bishop David L. Toups

"The king appointed for them a daily ration from the king's choice food and from the wine which he drank, and appointed that they should be educated three years, at the end of which they were to enter the king's personal service. Now among them from the sons of Judah were Daniel, Hananiah, Mishael and Azariah. Then the commander of the officials assigned new names to them; and to Daniel he assigned the name Belteshazzar, to Hananiah Shadrach, to Mishael Meshach and to Azariah Abed-nego" (Daniel 1:5-8).

This is not just the motto of the Boy Scouts but should also be the motto of every Christian. Being at the table for nourishment gives us the strength to get through the challenges of life. The Scripture above speaks of the four young exiles who were strengthened and nourished at their table and by their communion with each other. They had no idea of what future challenges would come: Daniel in the lion's dean and the three young men would be thrown in the fiery furnace.

As we know, all four were spared, and their preparation ahead of time prepared them for what they could not have imagined.

Their life of prayer and fellowship was foundational to get them through the challenges of life. Let's not underestimate that every meal is like one more layer of a foundation that is being laid, so that our houses will not collapse under the storms that inevitably come.

Day 25

I REALLY JUST WANTED TO ENCOURAGE YOU
Dr. John R. Adolph

"And the Lord said, Simon, Simon, behold, Satan hath desired to have you, that he may sift you as wheat: But I have prayed for thee, that thy faith fail not: and when thou art converted, strengthen thy brethren" (Luke 22:31-32)

Not long ago, a Father took his high school kids to dinner. While they sat wondering what this whole "let's go to dinner" thing was all about, the oldest son asked his father directly, "Dad, what's all of this about? Are you okay?" To which the Father replied, "Yes. I'm doing great, but I'm doing this because I really just wanted to encourage you." You see, the youngest child was a freshman and would encounter the feeling of starting over from the bottom again. The oldest child was a senior and would have to face substantial life choices and would need some wisdom from him along the way to make the best decisions possible. Though both kids would need different things, they would both need to find encouragement from him along the way, as is the case with Peter in this passage. Jesus knows what's ahead of him and wants to encourage him along the way. Can you remember a time when you needed a word of encouragement? Just a boost from someone who you loved and could depend on? Here's some chatter that matters from our communal table of faith: God did not bring you this far to leave you! He is with you, and so are your brothers and sisters in the Lord Jesus Christ who celebrate your perseverance in the faith!

Day 26

FAILURE IS NOT AN OPTION
Bishop David L. Toups

"Now when evening came, Jesus was reclining at the table with the twelve disciples. As they were eating, He said, 'Truly I say to you that one of you will betray Me'" (Matthew 26:20-21).

"Houston, we have a problem." Who can forget those alarming words spoken by the crew of Apollo 13 (or as my Dad would call it, Tom Hanks' mission). Despite their many setbacks and challenges, they did not give up and their recurring refrain was that "failure is not an option." As we strive to get back to the table as families, there will be setbacks, awkward moments, and maybe even someone storming away from the table or even not showing up.

Please don't fret or give up when this happens. We are in good company with Jesus who experienced such abandonment on the night of the Last Supper.

A good initiative is to have a game plan. Invite family members to reflect on the highlight and the challenge of their day (highs and lows) and go around the table sharing from the heart. Another wonderful reflection is to ask, did you help someone today? And be creative, talk about current events, sports and entertainment.

Don't give up! Persevere, keep showing up, keep forgiving, and keep inviting your family to the meal knowing that it is about the dividends that this will pay in the future, and not about short-term setbacks.

Day 27

LIFTING A FORK DOESN'T MAKE YOU STRONG
Dr. John R. Adolph

"And the Lord said, Simon, Simon, behold, Satan hath desired to have you, that he may sift you as wheat: But I have prayed for thee, that thy faith fail not: and when thou art converted, strengthen thy brethren" (Luke 22:31-32)

Let's agree on this one thing: When your season of struggle concludes, you always end up stronger than before it began. In short, if you believe in Jesus Christ, like a tea bag in boiling water, we conclude that the hotter the water, the stronger the brew. In short, our struggles make us stronger. With this in mind, Jesus tells Peter, "...when thou art converted, strengthen your brethren." A better translation of this phrase would read like this: When you get back up on your feet, use the strength you have gained from your struggle to help another believer who is struggling. The good news is that your season of strife does not last forever! It will end, and when it comes, a new season will arise where you are spiritually stronger and wiser than you are now. The Lord reminds us that I did not bring you out of your season for you. I brought you out so that you would have the strength to help those at the table who are struggling right now! Can you hear the Lord's voice yet? God says, "Just like I have helped you, I want you to help them!" With this in mind, remember that lifting a fork will not make you strong, but enduring your trial will! With your strength, help those near you that need it!

Day 28

LOVE TILL IT HURTS
Bishop David L. Toups

"It was just before the Passover Festival. Jesus knew that the hour had come for him to leave this world and go to the Father. Having loved his own who were in the world, he loved them to the end. The evening meal was in progress, and the devil had already prompted Judas, the son of Simon Iscariot, to betray Jesus. Jesus knew that the Father had put all things under his power, and that he had come from God and was returning to God;" (John 13:1-3)

For our families to experience renewal, it will take some blood, sweat, and tears. We know that it cost Jesus his life as "He loved us to the end." Love is ultimately self-sacrificial as modelled by Our Lord on the Cross. In marriage the "two become one" but two strong wills remain – I can only imagine that such sacrificial love in marriage and family entails a lot of death to self.

Parenting in the 21st century is filled with challenges, and for those who do so as single parents, it is nothing short of heroic. The added sacrifices of caring for aging parents, or parents still caring for adult children, none of this is easy. Only by God's grace can we love as He loves us. May we learn to love even when it hurts, to forgive when we have been hurt, and to keep showing up at the table even when we don't feel like it.

Day 29

I OWE HIM THIS, AND SO DO YOU
Dr. John R. Adolph

"And being in Bethany in the house of Simon, the leper, as he sat at meat, there came a woman having an alabaster box of ointment of spikenard very precious; and she brake the box, and poured it on his head" (Mark 14:3)

At the core of Jesus' life on earth was a table. It is safe to say that the entire life of Jesus Christ on earth was seen heading to a table, sharing with someone at a table, or leaving a table. The table mentioned in today's devotional lesson is a table that paints a beautiful portrait of a woman who shows up to bless Him before He can get to the cross because she reaches a point of realization that she owes Him more than she could ever repay Him. In the Baptist Church, worship can often be very expressive. What is meant by this is that there are times that parishioners seated in the pews will shout words of acclamation to God in praise and worship. One Sunday, a woman was heard shouting, "I owe Him this, and so do you!" This woman carrying this alabaster box is Mary, Lazarus's sister, and she realizes that she owes the Lord more than she could ever repay Him. The difference between a mature Christian and someone young in the faith is simple. Those who are young are waiting for their next blessing. God owes them! A mature believer knows that God owes us nothing. If anything, we owe Him everything because He's given us so much!

Day 30

SELFLESS SERVICE
Bishop David L. Toups

"...he got up from the meal, took off his outer clothing, and wrapped a towel around his waist. After that, he poured water into a basin and began to wash his disciples' feet, drying them with the towel that was wrapped around him. [...] "Now that I, your Lord and Teacher, have washed your feet, you also should wash one another's feet. I have set you an example that you should do as I have done for you. Very truly I tell you, no servant is greater than his master, nor is a messenger greater than the one who sent him. Now that you know these things, you will be blessed if you do them." (John 13:4-5; 14-17)

We reenact this beautiful moment of the Last Supper when Jesus washes the feet of the Apostles at the Holy Thursday Liturgy. Sometimes it is called Maundy Thursday coming from the Latin word *Mandatum* translated as "mandate" or "commandment." For after Jesus humbled Himself and washed their feet, He told them "as I have done for you, so you must do". This meal reminds us to be selfless servants of our brothers and sisters in our community. Service begins in the home to spouse, children, and sick loved ones. Then it expands to the needs of our church community and then beyond the walls of the church to serve the poor and homeless, the needy immigrant, as well as our local civic organizations.

The Maundy Thursday meal sends us forth to wash the feet of our brothers and sisters, and hopefully will help us lead others back to the table as we reach out to them as their selfless servants.

Day 31

WALK IN'S AREN'T ALWAYS WELCOMED
Dr. John R. Adolph

"And being in Bethany in the house of Simon the leper, as he sat at meat, there came a woman having an alabaster box of ointment of spikenard very precious; and she brake the box, and poured it on his head" (Mark 14:4)

It's a sign you often see when entering physical nurture and wellness shops. You walk into a nail shop for a pedicure or manicure, and the sign reads Walk In's Welcome. Are you looking for a nice haircut? Not a problem. Find a neighboring barbershop, and as soon as you reach the door, the sign reads "Walk In's Welcome." But it should be clear that walk-ins are only sometimes welcome. Some tables won't include you because you just don't fit in the minds of those who make up the table. Mary is the nameless woman in the passage. She is not invited to the dinner that is taking place in the text, but she asks herself. It is interesting to note that she, unlike the others, did not come to get a blessing from the Lord; she came to bestow one. She brought spikenard, the most expensive aromatic fragrances of the day, to anoint Him. She brought Him her best because when she needed God, the Lord gave her His best in the presence and personality of His only begotten Son, our Savior, Jesus Christ. Here's the moral of today's devotional: some tables may reject you. But do not take the rejection personally. Shake the dust from your feet, give God your best, and leave the rest to Him.

Day 32

RIGHTEOUS ANGER
Bishop David L. Toups

"And He found in the temple those who were selling oxen and sheep and doves, and the money changers seated at their tables. And He made a scourge of cords, and drove them all out of the temple, with the sheep and the oxen; and He poured out the coins of the money changers and overturned their tables;" (John 2:14-15)

We have seen many examples of Jesus lovingly sitting at the table welcoming sinners, enjoying His family and friends, and delighting in the great Mediterranean cuisine.

But in this scripture, we find something quite different, He isn't reclining at table, He is overturning the tables of the money changers in the Temple. "Don't you know that my Father's house is a house of prayer." There is such a thing that we call righteous anger when our reactions are less than calm or gentle in order to make an important point.

This is a prophetic action meant to teach a lesson. We need prophets in our world today and sometimes even expressing our feelings with intensity.

Our world and society need us to speak up and turn over some tables as Jesus did. Now obviously we do such things peacefully, but there is also a time and place when we are called to speak out. Our community needs us to speak out against racism, gender ideologies, domestic violence, abortion, homelessness, and so many injustices that we see around us all the time. Let us work together and straighten the tables of our homes, schools and churches, in order to change our community for the good.

Day 33

SHE SHOULDN'T BE THE ONLY ONE WITH A DISH

Dr. John R. Adolph

"And being in Bethany in the house of Simon the leper, as he sat at meat, there came a woman having an alabaster box of ointment of spikenard very precious; and she brake the box, and poured it on his head" (Mark 14:5)

It was a family potluck supper, and it promised to be exciting! The general understanding was that everyone was supposed to bring something. Children were to get the ice because they don't usually cook. Teens were to bring sodas because they knew what flavors they consumed. Adults were to bring the sides and meats. After all, they are the real family cooks. Doors open at Ma Dear's house, and she's cooked everything but waits on the unique dishes and casseroles from the family. And nobody had cooked a thing except for her baby girl with her famous smoked turkey mac and cheese specialty. It was then that Ma Dear shouted her words of rebuke. She said, "Y'all know she shouldn't be the only one with a dish!" The root of this lesson presses the same issue. In the passage above, Mary should not be the only one with something to contribute. Yet she is! If you are at the Lord's communal table, you don't just show up to receive things from Him. It would be best if you showed up with something to give. Your praise, give Him that! Your adoration, give Him that! Your communal serve, give Him that! He is so worthy of the honor, the gratitude, and the glory! In the hearts and minds of every believer, there are none like Him!

Day 34

FOLLOW ME
Bishop David L. Toups

"As Jesus went on from there, he saw a man named Matthew sitting at the tax collector's booth. "Follow me," he told him, and Matthew got up and followed him" (Matthew 9:9).

One of my favorite paintings is by a renaissance artist named Caravaggio entitled the "Call of Matthew". It depicts Mathew the taxcollector sitting at the table with his ill-gotten fortune stacked up in front of him. Then the Light of Christ breaks into his life; the contrast in the painting is striking as Matthew sits in his darkness and the light from Jesus radiates forth. I invite you to google this painting and place yourself in the seat of Matthew and allow the light and warmth of Christ's love and forgiveness envelope you and listen in your heart for His voice to say to you "Follow me". We are called to get up from the table of our own complacency and begin or continue our journey to becoming a saint like Matthew.

It is a life's journey and a daily decision for each of us to receive Jesus' love, mercy, and strength. This scriptural scene is also the basis of the motto of Pope Francis' *Miserando atque eligendo*, which can be translated: with eyes of mercy, he chose me.

Jesus gazes upon each of us with His merciful eyes and He has chosen us to be His followers.

Let us heed His call and Follow Him!

Day 35

IT WAS THE BEST I HAD TO OFFER
Dr. John R. Adolph

"And Jesus said, Let her alone; why trouble ye her? She hath wrought a good work on me" (Mark 14:6)

When we pause to consider the table in the passage above, it presses us to consider what giving God our best looks like. With this in mind, have you ever noticed that we want the best of everything? We do not desire polyester; we want silk. We do not look to purchase a cubic zirconia; we want a diamond. And we do not wish to buy pleather; we enjoy an excellent grade of leather. Why? We want the best. However, when it comes to serving God as a community of faith, we tend to think that God should accept whatever we give Him, and nothing could be further from the truth. Take a moment to read the passage above and consider that Mary brought Jesus spikenard in her alabaster box. It was a costly aromatic fragrance that was worth the annual salary of a centurion soldier. Here's today's devotional lesson: She brought the Lord the best she had to offer. Take a moment and survey your soul. Ask yourself this question: Am I giving God the best I can offer? If you feel a sense of spiritual conviction because you know that you could provide the Lord with much more, then start today by doing your best for Him because when it comes to blessing you, He has given you the best that He has to offer in His Son, our Savior Jesus Christ!

Day 36

THE CHARCOAL FIRE
Bishop David L. Toups

"When they landed, they saw a fire of burning coals there with fish on it, and some bread" (John 21:9).

There are only two places where the words "charcoal fire" appear in the Gospels. The first is in the courtyard of the high priest where St. Peter denied Jesus three times, and now the second time on the shores of Galilee where the risen Christ forgives and heals this wound in Peter's soul.

We know how strong muscle memory is and how our sense of smell can bring us back immediately to both good and bad memories.

We can imagine Peter walking up the beach seeing and smelling the charcoal fire where our risen Savior was preparing the meal. As he is flooded with his own guilt, Jesus asks three times "Peter, do you love me?" Peter's threefold profession of faith and love and the mission Jesus entrusted to him, "feed my sheep", was the healing he needed to overcome his sins of his past. In the same manner, Jesus wants to help us let go of our mistakes and sins so that we can move forward with great freedom.

And notice, it all happened once again at a meal – let's get back to the table.

Day 37

BIG BOSS HOT SAUCE
Dr. John R. Adolph

"She hath done what she could: she is come aforehand to anoint my body to the burying" (Mark 14:8)

One thing that often damages the table of Christian fellowship the world over is the underlying tug of war-that deals with who gets the big seat at the table. Here's the truth: Some people will only participate if they possess a particular position or a reasonable portion of power. The Urban Dictionary refers to people of this sort on this wise, "big boss, hot sauce." However, at the heart of the Christian community worldwide, there is only one person, one personality that merits a chief seat at the head of our communal table, and His name is Jesus Christ. When Mary approaches the table in our text, she is not there to pay homage or obeisance to anyone but the Lord. The story's moral is this: He alone is worthy of our honor, worship, and praise. Imagine, for a moment, what our community would look like if we all sought to lift the Lord in our efforts, through our energy, with our excellence. What could we accomplish if we were to celebrate our King and work to unite His Kingdom on earth? It would reveal the greatest manifestation of God's glory the world has ever seen from the body of Christ, the Church.

Day 38

THE 153

Bishop David L. Toups

"Jesus said to them, "Bring some of the fish you have just caught." So Simon Peter climbed back into the boat and dragged the net ashore. It was full of large fish, 153, but even with so many the net was not torn. Jesus said to them, "Come and have breakfast." None of the disciples dared ask him, "Who are you?" They knew it was the Lord. Jesus came, took the bread and gave it to them, and did the same with the fish. This was now the third time Jesus appeared to his disciples after he was raised from the dead" (John 21:10-14).

I love a good hearty breakfast like a Denney's Grand Slam, but can you imagine how great the breakfast that Jesus prepared for the Apostles with 153 fish? So strange that St. John writes in the detail of the exact number of fish, isn't it? It is a great detail that teaches us something very important. In Jesus' day, it was understood that there were 153 different species of fish in the sea. The point is that the followers of Christ are meant to come from every race, culture, language, and background. We are meant to be a universal church, or as we say "catholic" – which is Greek word meaning "of the whole." The tables at our churches are meant to be places for all peoples.

Let's all be challenged to pray and worship in our churches with the 153. How I love to attend services across Southeast Texas and look out at faces that represent the great cultural diversity of our community of faith. Come to the table!

Day 39

THE BEST MEAL EVER
Dr. John R. Adolph

"Verily I say unto you, Wheresoever this gospel shall be preached throughout the whole world, this also that she hath done shall be spoken of for a memorial of her" (Mark 14:9)

You only remember some of the tables you have shared in your life. The company was okay, the service was lousy, and the food was submerged in a sense of blah. On the contrary, there are other times that you dine, and what was prepared is so unique that you refuse to leave the leftovers. But what makes the best meal ever is when you share a table with someone for the last time. There's just something about a final meal that makes it the best meal ever. Here in our passage of study, we encounter the last meal of our Master before He journeys to the cross. It was His previous gathering before He would lay down His life for the sins of the world. Yet, at His table were men who were clueless about what He would do with and through their lives in days to come. There was a woman with a box of perfume who desired to anoint Him, and at least two of the Disciples present wanted positions of power. However, amid it all, from this table rises a sacrifice that would change the world forever. You see, what makes a meal the best is when you realize that you have gathered for the final time with someone you love and, more importantly, someone who loves you. Here's a probing devotional query to grapple with as we look in retrospect at the table in our text today. If you could have been at the table with Jesus before He made His way to the cross, what would you have said to Him? Believe it or not, there is still time to pray your thoughts to Him. He is listening.

Day 40

DO YOU LOVE ME?

Bishop David L. Toups

"When they had finished eating, Jesus said to Simon Peter, 'Simon son of John, do you love me more than these?' 'Yes, Lord,' he said, 'you know that I love you.' Jesus said, 'Feed my lambs.' Again Jesus said, 'Simon son of John, do you love me?' He answered, 'Yes, Lord, you know that I love you.' Jesus said, 'Take care of my sheep.' The third time he said to him, 'Simon son of John, do you love me?' Peter was hurt because Jesus asked him the third time, 'Do you love me?' He said, 'Lord, you know all things; you know that I love you.' Jesus said, 'Feed my sheep. Very truly I tell you, when you were younger you dressed yourself and went where you wanted; but when you are old you will stretch out your hands, and someone else will dress you and lead you where you do not want to go.' Jesus said this to indicate the kind of death by which Peter would glorify God. Then he said to him, 'Follow me!'" (John 21:15-19).

As Jesus invites Peter into a threefold profession of faith and love, the first time he asks the question it is longer than the second two times he asks. Not just "Do you love me?" but "Do you love me <u>more than these</u>?" I have often reflected on what "more than these" refers to. Was Jesus pointing to the other Apostles, "Do you love me more than these?" or was He speaking more broadly referring to his family, career, possessions, and reputation, "Do you love me more than these?"

The answer is "yes" to both, Jesus is inviting Peter (and us) to love Him before and above all things.

When we love God first and foremost, then all of our others loves fall in place and are well-ordered.

From time to time, we need to be challenged with the same question and make sure we are not making idols of people or possessions when we put them ahead of God. And all of this happened at a meal – Let's get back to the Table.

Day 41

THE SWEET AROMA FROM THE KITCHEN
Dr. John R. Adolph

"Verily I say unto you, Wheresoever this gospel shall be preached throughout the whole world, this also that she hath done shall be spoken of for a memorial of her" (Mark 14:9)

In most cases, if a table is present, there could be a kitchen in nearby proximity. And you know what that means, don't you? The empirical blessing of smell finds the hidden horizons of pots and pans of what's soon to come. At the table in the passage, there is an added aroma in the air. It is perhaps coming from the kitchen, but it is not supper being prepared; it is a sacrifice being produced. It is the sweet aroma of spikenard. It is the oil used for the coronation of a King.

Mary uses this oil at the table in our passage because, in her eyes, Jesus is not just some Jewish revolutionary whose mission field has seen better days. He is her King in her heart, and she treats Him as such. At tables of religious belief around the world, people see Jesus differently. Some see Him as a Prophet, while others view Him as a Jewish troublemaker. Still, many see Him as a miracle worker, while others remember him as the guy from Nazareth who was crucified. However, at the table of a believing Christian, He is so much more! He is our rock, our redeemer, and the restorer of hope! He is our peace, portion, provision, and protector. He is our Lord, Savior, God, guide, and gracious friend! He is our King!

Day 42

INSIDE THE CUP
Bishop David L. Toups

"When Jesus had finished speaking, a Pharisee invited him to eat with him; so he went in and reclined at the table. But the Pharisee was surprised when he noticed that Jesus did not first wash before the meal. Then the Lord said to him, "Now then, you Pharisees clean the outside of the cup and dish, but inside you are full of greed and wickedness. You foolish people! Did not the one who made the outside make the inside also? But now as for what is inside you—be generous to the poor, and everything will be clean for you" (Luke 11:37-41).

We all know that it is so important to have clean dishes when we sit down to dine. It makes no sense to clean the outside of the dish only, especially since the most important area to clean is the inside of the cup and dish lest we get sick. But the lesson Jesus is teaching here is not just about doing the dishes, He is talking about the interior of our souls. He is admonishing the community to not just follow the externals of religion and ignore the interior renewal and cleansing that really matters.

I also like to use the image of the car wash. If all we do is run our car through the wash but never clean the inside of the car, we are forgetting to clean the most important part – where we are! We need to clean the windows so we can see better, get rid of the empty fast food bags, and pick up the old soda cans and french-fries under the seats. In the same ways let's prepare our hearts and souls before we come to the Table of the Lord every Sunday because it is the perfect time to be reconciled to God and to one another!

Day 43

IT'S LIKE MUSIC TO MY EARS
Dr. John R. Adolph

"And they, continuing daily with one accord in the temple, and breaking bread from house to house, did eat their meat with gladness and singleness of heart" (Acts 2:26)

Suppose you have never heard it before; it can resemble the sound of music. What is it you ask? The sound of pots, pans, plates, and dishes clicking and tapping in the kitchen. When you are hungry, and the table is nearly ready to receive those prepared to dine, it is like the old saying, "It's like music to my ears!" Almost gone are the days when a family makes time to dine together at the table. Yet, when the family of faith came together, as recorded by Luke in the Book of Acts, it is precisely what they did. The Biblical record reflects that they went "...house to house with one accord..." The term accord is a musical idiom suggesting that, like keys on a piano, though all different, they can make beautiful music when brought together skillfully. Nothing can bring us together harmoniously like food, faith, and fellowship. These three, when shared, can be like music to your ears. Here's an excellent question: what are you waiting on? Bring your family together and get to the table!

Day 44

ALTAR FRONTAL
Bishop David L. Toups

"Now the tax collectors and sinners were all gathering around to hear Jesus. But the Pharisees and the teachers of the law muttered, "This man welcomes sinners and eats with them" (Luke 15:1-2).

It is so beautiful to see how open Jesus is to the marginalized, and a little scary to see his reaction to the self-righteous religious people of his day.

The self-righteous do not believe they need God and are judgmental to those they deem to be unclean or different.

Thus, Our Lord comes to our <u>rescue</u> and invites us to the table. Jesus wears as a badge of honor their words of harsh judgement against Him: "This man welcomes sinners and eats with them." In fact, to drive the point home, the great bishop of north Africa, St. Augustine, said that these words should be carved into the marble of every altar in every church around the world. What a beautiful idea! It would serve as a reminder to us that we all need our Savior to save us who are sinners, and it would serve as an invitation to those who are afraid to return to Jesus because of their sins of the past or simply their absence from the community for many years.

Let's remind them that "This man welcomes sinners and eats with them!"

Day 45

LET US BREAK BREAD TOGETHER
Dr. John R. Adolph

"And they, continuing daily with one accord in the temple, and breaking bread from house to house, did eat their meat with gladness and singleness of heart" (Acts 2:26)

Did you know that the purpose of a table was to foster, push, and promote a sense of family and togetherness? Dr. Edward P. Wimberly, retired professor of Pastoral Care at the Interdenominational Theological Center, said, "A table was the place of communal unity and togetherness and the heart of every family." If Wimberly is correct, it's time for us to get back to the table. When Luke writes the book of Acts, he is careful to chronicle how the church grew and how the table was the centerpiece of their fellowship. Can you remember when the table was the centerpiece of family sitcoms? The Jeffersons had a table; Thelma, J-J, and Michael had a table on Good Times; Archie and Edith Bunker had a table. Returning to the table allows us the practice and privilege of breaking bread together as we share with each other and walk with God.

Day 46

THE PRODIGAL SON
Bishop David L. Toups

"But while he was still a long way off, his father saw him and was filled with compassion for him; he ran to his son, threw his arms around him and kissed him. The son said to him, 'Father, I have sinned against heaven and against you. I am no longer worthy to be called your son.' "But the father said to his servants, 'Quick! Bring the best robe and put it on him. Put a ring on his finger and sandals on his feet. Bring the fattened calf and kill it. Let's have a feast and celebrate. For this son of mine was dead and is alive again; he was lost and is found.' So they began to celebrate" (Luke 15:20-24).

Who among us is without fault or sin? We all make mistakes and turn our backs on God from time to time because we are a part of fallen humanity.

That is the whole point of Jesus coming to save us, because left to our own devices we cannot follow Him. Even with His grace, we mess up sometimes. We are the prodigal son who so desperately need to return to our loving Father who immediately wants to embrace us and restore us to our dignity as His sons and daughters. He has prepared a banquet at His table and doesn't want us to keep ourselves away from his generous mercy and love. Sometimes I hear people say to me that they have not returned to church because the roof would collapse or lightning would strike. To which I respond... get over yourself (LOL). There is nothing we have done that our magnificent and generous Father is not willing to forgive. Like the prodigal son we simply have to keep returning to His loving arms.

Day 47

YOU DO THE POTLUCK NEXT TIME
Dr. John R. Adolph

"And they, continuing daily with one accord in the temple, and breaking bread from house to house, did eat their meat with gladness and singleness of heart" (Acts 2:26)

You do not know what you're missing if you have never attended one. What is it you ask? A potluck supper. If you are unfamiliar with it, let's say it is just like a huge buffet line made up of all your favorite foods, prepared by people who are skillfully blessed with culinary expertise and some dishes you have never tried. Still, once you taste them, you will beg for the recipe. Listen, there's nothing like a potluck supper. When you read Acts 2:46-48, it gives the feel of a potluck meal. The idea of "... breaking bread from house to house..." provides that vibe. However, examining this passage allows you to ask yourself, "When was the last time I had family and friends over for a meal like this?" The sweet fellowship, laughter, genuine fun, and food that's been prepared can bring about healing and blessing that can only come from a table. So here's an excellent question to ask at a moment like this, "What are you waiting on? You do the potluck next time."

Day 48

THE BEGRUDGING BROTHER
Bishop David L. Toups

"'But when this son of yours who has squandered your property with prostitutes comes home, you kill the fattened calf for him!' 'My son,' the father said, 'you are always with me, and everything I have is yours. But we had to celebrate and be glad, because this brother of yours was dead and is alive again; he was lost and is found.'" (Luke 15:30-32).

We can either receive the Lord's beautiful gift of hospitality by resting in the arms of the Father as did the prodigal son, or we can be like the begrudging brother who rejects the fattened calf. The older brother never understood that the Father wanted to be in a loving relationship with him all along, rather he just followed the rules out of a sense of duty without any real meaning, leaving him bitter when his no-good baby brother returned. Rather than rejoicing that the lost was found, he pouted and grumbled refusing even to sit at the table together. We must guard our hearts from the same attitude when someone returns to church after years of being far from the Lord.

No matter what they have done, or injured along the way, if their return and conversion is genuine, we should rejoice that the person who was dead has been brought to life again in Christ. This is the welcome we should give upon their return – rejoice and be glad they have come back to the table!

Day 49

THERE'S NOTHING LIKE MOMMA'S SMOTHERED PORK CHOPS
Dr. John R. Adolph

"And they, continuing daily with one accord in the temple, and breaking bread from house to house, did eat their meat with gladness and singleness of heart" (Acts 2:26)

Growing up with a mother who stayed in the kitchen, there was always a weekly menu we could look forward to. Mondays brought leftovers from Sunday. Tuesdays was always a casserole that would stretch. Wednesdays could be a total surprise. Fridays were made for fried fish. But, Thursdays could bless you like crazy because it was smothered pork chops and gravy. There was no such thing as a veggie plate at the home front. A plate had to have some meat on it to be complete. In Acts 2, as the chapter concludes, Luke shares that as the church grew in the faith, they also grew in fellowship. This included but was not limited to, meat being served at the table. This is always important because it reminds us that something had to die for those eating the meal to live. There was nothing like those smothered pork chops; there is nothing like knowing that our Lord would sacrifice His life so that we might live.

Day 50

COME ON DOWN
Bishop David L. Toups

"When Jesus reached the spot, he looked up and said to him, "Zacchaeus, come down immediately. I must stay at your house today." So he came down at once and welcomed him gladly. All the people saw this and began to mutter, "He has gone to be the guest of a sinner." But Zacchaeus stood up and said to the Lord, "Look, Lord! Here and now I give half of my possessions to the poor, and if I have cheated anybody out of anything, I will pay back four times the amount." Jesus said to him, "Today salvation has come to this house, because this man, too, is a son of Abraham. For the Son of Man came to seek and to save the lost." (Luke 19: 5-10).

When the late Bob Barker called on contestants to "come on down" you would have thought they had already won a million dollars. With giddy joy, they would run down the aisle with arms failing as they came forward.

Zacchaeus received the same invitation from the Lord to "come on down" and he joyfully does so coming down from the tree to welcome Christ to his home.

He was invited to participate in the greatest adventure of life – the journey of Christianity and the path of holiness.

And the "price was right" too, because the invitation of Jesus is free to all who turn to Him. Salvation is a gift that Christ won for us that we cannot merit or attain on our own strength. Pope Francis reminded the young people at World Youth Day: "Nothing in life is free, except the love of Jesus" (August 5, 2023)

Once this love is accepted, we can "come on down" like Zacchaeus, and then no matter what the cost of discipleship is, we don't mind paying because we are in communion with Jesus and we don't mind "laying down our lives" nor "taking up our Crosses" to follow Him.

Day 51

WHEN HAPPENINGS FROM THE TABLE MAKE YOU HAPPY
Dr. John R. Adolph

"And they, continuing daily with one accord in the temple, and breaking bread from house to house, did eat their meat with gladness and singleness of heart" (Acts 2:26)

Have you ever found your way to the table overwhelmed with hunger, and what was on it blessed you to the point that it changed your attitude? If it's never happened to you, it may be because you have never really been hungry. The story was told of two teenagers who returned home from football practice. They walked into the house, agitated, frustrated, and starving. But things soon changed when they arrived in the kitchen because, to their surprise, homemade pizza awaited them. Frowns became smiles because what was on the table altered their attitude. In the passage listed above, something similar takes place. The text says, "... They did eat their meat with gladness..." The word gladness translates into the term happy. Therefore, the people from the passage were made comfortable because of what was happening on the table. Here's a devotional prayer to conclude this reflective moment. May the Lord of heaven always bless those who gather at your table and may be favor and fill you with what comes from it. In Jesus' name. Amen.

Day 52

RE-COGNIZE HIM
Bishop David L. Toups

"When he was at the table with them, he took bread, gave thanks, broke it and began to give it to them. Then their eyes were opened and they recognized him, and he disappeared from their sight. They asked each other, "Were not our hearts burning within us while he talked with us on the road and opened the Scriptures to us?" (Luke 24:30-32).

The disciples on the road to Emmaus have the encounter of their lives as they sit down at table with the risen Christ, whom they do not yet recognize. It was not until He did the very familiar action of taking bread, giving thanks, breaking it and giving it to them. Then Jesus disappeared from them, but He was not gone for he remained with them in the Eucharist – Jesus was there under the guise of Bread just as he promised in John chapter six and the accounts of the Last Supper. In our Catholic Tradition we believe that Jesus is present Body, Blood, Soul, and Divinity in Holy Communion in order to feed, nourish, heal, and comfort our souls at every Mass.

We just need to "recognized Him in the breaking of the Bread" as the disciples did on the road to Emmaus. Re-cognize means to "know again", may we open the eyes of our hearts every time we approach the table of the Lord so that our hearts may burn within us and then return home as the disciples did by sharing the good news that Jesus indeed is risen from the dead.

Day 53

GOD'S FAVORITE NUMBER
Dr. John R. Adolph

"And they, continuing daily with one accord in the temple, and breaking bread from house to house, did eat their meat with gladness and singleness of heart" (Acts 2:26)

When scripture numerics is studied, it's clear that God not only numbers things but also makes numbers count. In making numbers count, every number in the Bible has a meaning. For example, two is the number of unity; three is the number of the trinity, four is the number of universality, five is the number of gratuity, and so forth. But what is God's favorite number? Here's the revelation: His favorite number has to be one. It is the number of unity. The meaning of "....singleness of heart..." is mentioned in the verse above. A better translation would be rendered like this, "... The people at the table had one heart..." What a beautiful portrait of faith and family this truly is. They are one in their humanity, one in their community, and one as it relates to faith and family. They were one! It's no wonder the church grew so rapidly. The people were one. And it's no wonder a family is most substantial at the table. It is the place of oneness.

Day 54

USE OUR WEAKNESSES
Bishop David L. Toups

"When Jesus looked up and saw a great crowd coming toward him, he said to Philip, "Where shall we buy bread for these people to eat?" 6 He asked this only to test him, for he already had in mind what he was going to do. Philip answered him, "It would take more than half a year's wages [a] to buy enough bread for each one to have a bite!" Another of his disciples, Andrew, Simon Peter's brother, spoke up, 9 "Here is a boy with five small barley loaves and two small fish, but how far will they go among so many?" (John 6:5-8).

We often think we need to serve God from our own strength, or that because we go to Church on Sunday and participate in the life of our faith communities that we are uber-Christians.

Nothing could be farther from the truth. God wants us to come to Him in our poverty – "all we have are a few loaves and fishes."

Then Jesus can take what little we have and work miracles through us. It is He who is our strength as St. Paul remind us (2 Corinthians 12:10). It is Jesus' mother Mary that also reminds us in Luke 1:49: "The Almighty has done great things for me, and Holy is His name."

We just need to get out of the way and let God work through us more powerfully than we could imagine.

Now to the second point: we come to Church, are involved in our faith communities, and pray daily not because we are the best of Christians, but because we are the weakest of all – we simply recognize that we need it for "without Christ we can do nothing" (John 15:5). We come to the table not because we are full, but because we are starving for Him.

Day 55

SOMETHING TO SHOUT ABOUT
Dr. John R. Adolph

"Praising God, and having favour with all the people. And the Lord added to the church daily such as should be saved" (Acts 2:47)

There are times when fans at a sporting event shout. It expresses excellent joy over something that just happened: a home run, a touchdown, a hole-in-one. However, when it regards people of faith, when should we shout? According to Acts 2:47, we should "praise God" when we come together at a table with everything in common. This makes us have to raise the question, why? Here's the simple answer: it is a miracle every time we set our differences aside and decide to love one another and share in unity. It reminds us how things will be in heaven when we finally make it there. But until that day comes, we shout and celebrate while we are here on earth as we share as a faith family in the Lord Jesus Christ. The next time you gather at the table with your family, you should ask them to celebrate the God of heaven with you as you prepare to break bread together.

Day 56

LIVING BREAD
Bishop David L. Toups

"I am the bread of life. Your ancestors ate the manna in the wilderness, yet they died. But here is the bread that comes down from heaven, which anyone may eat and not die. I am the living bread that came down from heaven. Whoever eats this bread will live forever. This bread is my flesh, which I will give for the life of the world." (John 6:48-51).

Isn't it amazing to see the foreshadowing in the Old Testament of Christ's Eucharistic Presence? God fed the Israelites during their exodus in a miraculous fashion so that they would not die. The manna could not be explained and at times it wasn't even appreciated, yet for forty years "Bread from Heaven" rained down upon the chosen people. We believe that this Bread from Heaven continues to fall upon us at the Table of the Lord, but as opposed to our ancestor in the faith, "whoever eats this bread will live forever." We are in our exile right now on a journey to the Promised Land, as so He feeds us with the finest wheat. Like Jesus' own body, the grains are crushed and ground in order to become nourishment and give life to others. For over two thousand years, we have gathered at the Table of the Lord so that we can continue to be fed by the Manna from above, so that we will not die of hunger in the desert and arrive safely to our heavenly destination.

Day 57

OUR TABLE NEEDS A FEW MORE SEATS
Dr. John R. Adolph

"Praising God, and having favour with all the people. And the Lord added to the church daily such as should be saved" (Acts 2:47)

Acts two records what took place on Pentecost and the growth of the Lord's church that resulted from the presence and potency of the Holy Spirit. The most exciting news about the development was that the table was its centerpiece, and families and households from the community surrounded it. On a day when pews are empty and churches are closing, it is refreshing to read that our first church grew to where it needed more seats at the table. This occurred because families came together to celebrate the person of Jesus Christ, the Son of the living God. The need for more seats suggests that all empty seats have already been taken. It indicates that the grace that we have been blessed with is also needed by others who are just like we used to be. Here's the best news of the day: There is always room at the table of the family of God.....always!

Day 58

REAL FOOD/REAL DRINK
Bishop David L. Toups

"Then the Jews began to argue sharply among themselves, "How can this man give us his flesh to eat?" Jesus said to them, "Very truly I tell you, unless you eat the flesh of the Son of Man and drink his blood, you have no life in you. Whoever eats my flesh and drinks my blood has eternal life, and I will raise them up at the last day. For my flesh is real food and my blood is real drink. Whoever eats my flesh and drinks my blood remains in me, and I in them. Just as the living Father sent me and I live because of the Father, so the one who feeds on me will live because of me. This is the bread that came down from heaven. Your ancestors ate manna and died, but whoever feeds on this bread will live forever." (John 6:52-58).

Junk food may taste good momentarily, but it can never nourish us. We need real food/real drink to be sustained. Those are Christ's words today reminding us that he is the real thing. He nourishes us in both Word and Sacrament to strengthen us in holiness.

The Word of God in the Sacred Scriptures equips us for life and teaches us how to live. We all know the acronym for BIBLE: Basic Instructions Before Leaving Earth!

After we unpack the Scriptures as our services, we then transition to the Sacrament of the Altar. Then like two halves of a great football game, we move from the table of the Word to the table of the Lord so that He can feed us "for my flesh is real food and my blood real drink." This is no mere analogy but a reality.

Why and how is this possible many ask? Well, simply because Jesus said so, and He is the Real Deal! #ComeToTheTable.

Day 59

IT'S WHY THE CHURCH KEEPS ON GROWING
Dr. John R. Adolph

"Praising God, and having favour with all the people. And the Lord added to the church daily such as should be saved" (Acts 2:47).

As a younger Pastor, I used to think that church growth resulted from my morning sermon. A few years later, I thought people united with us because the choir sang the right songs. But, after really looking at what took place, I realized that church growth resulted from the blessing of the Lord, the fellowship of the saints, and the benefit of what was on the table. In short, we always grew greater when we shared with our family and friends in a spirit of communal fellowship where a table was involved. In short, there is something extraordinary, mystical, and monumental about what God does when we touch, agree, share, and gather at the table. Here's the secret to church growth: make sure that you keep the table of the Lord as the vital visible part of every family and every church in our community.

Day 60

WE ALL NEED BETHANY
Bishop David L. Toups

"Six days before the Passover, Jesus came to Bethany, where Lazarus lived, whom Jesus had raised from the dead. Here a dinner was given in Jesus' honor. Martha served, while Lazarus was among those reclining at the table with him. Then Mary took about a pint[a] of pure nard, an expensive perfume; she poured it on Jesus' feet and wiped his feet with her hair. And the house was filled with the fragrance of the perfume" (John 12:1-3).

One of Jesus favorite spots to relax was at the home of His friends: Martha, Mary, and Lazarus in Bethany.

Right before His passion, Jesus knew what He needed and He wanted the comfort of being at table with those who meant so much to Him. Just as He is always feeding them, He too needed the nourishment and comfort of friendship. We all need to get back to the table because we need a Bethany too. A place where we can relax, relate, and grow in our relationships. Such table fellowship doesn't happen overnight but is formed in the ups and downs of life, and over time the balm of friendship seals in the fragrance which strengthens us on the journey of life.

Likewise, our faith communities should also be like little Bethany's where we find comfort every week as we gather with fellow believers. This becomes for us a home where our souls find rest and our Good Shepherd "leads us to restful waters to revive our drooping spirit." (Ps 23:3).

We all need Bethany, after all Jesus did!

About the Authors

Dr. John R. Adolph is an honors graduate from the Interdenominal Theological Center, Morehouse School of Religion (MDIV) in Atlanta, Georgia. He is also an honors graduate of the Houston Graduate School of Theology (DMIN) in Houston, Texas. Dr. Adolph is the Pastor of Antioch Missionary Baptist Church in Beaumont, Texas, where he has served faithfully since 1996. He is a gifted teacher and preacher of the Word of God.

Bishop David Toups was ordained and installed the sixth bishop of the Diocese of Beaumont on August 21, 2020. Growing up as the youngest of three children in both Louisiana and Florida, he was ordained a priest in 1997 for the Diocese of St. Petersburg. He has previously served in parish ministry in Florida, in the office of the USCCB's Secretariat of Clergy, Consecrated Life, and Vocations in Washington, DC, and as a seminary professor, dean, and rector/president at St. Vincent de Paul Regional Seminary in Boynton Beach, Florida. He is now a proud Texan!

For more information email info@advbooks.com or visit our website at
www.advbookstore.com

Orlando, Florida, USA
"we bring dreams to life"™
www.advbookstore.com

Made in the USA
Columbia, SC
20 October 2023

24320786R10039